YOUR KNOWLEDGE HAS VALUE

Diane Botta

Aspects of Digital Advertising

Litterature Review

GRIN Verlag

Bibliografische Information der Deutschen Nationalbibliothek:

Die Deutsche Bibliothek verzeichnet diese Publikation in der Deutschen National-
bibliografie; detaillierte bibliografische Daten sind im Internet über http://dnb.d-
nb.de/ abrufbar.

Imprint:

Copyright © 2014 GRIN Verlag GmbH
Druck und Bindung: Books on Demand GmbH, Norderstedt Germany
ISBN: 978-3-656-73884-8

This book at GRIN:

http://www.grin.com/en/e-book/279990/aspects-of-digital-advertising

GRIN - Your knowledge has value

Der GRIN Verlag publiziert seit 1998 wissenschaftliche Arbeiten von Studenten, Hochschullehrern und anderen Akademikern als eBook und gedrucktes Buch. Die Verlagswebsite www.grin.com ist die ideale Plattform zur Veröffentlichung von Hausarbeiten, Abschlussarbeiten, wissenschaftlichen Aufsätzen, Dissertationen und Fachbüchern.

Visit us on the internet:

http://www.grin.com/

http://www.facebook.com/grincom

http://www.twitter.com/grin_com

Diane Botta

Litterature Review
Aspects of Digital Advertising

August 2014

According Carlota Perez in her book Technological revolutions and financial capital published in 2002, technological revolutions follow 4 main stages: interruption, frenzy, synergy and maturity. In 2009, Franck Mulhern evaluated the digital technological revolution has beginning its synergy stage. Indeed, the digital technology has proper funding sources to develop itself in the economy. According to the author, the traditional way of advertising was based on the process of delivering message to audiences as large as possible. Therefore, advertising, as a process aiming at targeting individuals to deliver brand message, is being transformed to data-driven contextualized brand message, freed of the link with news and entertainment. And, the implications of digital revolution are much deeper than the previous advertising revolution created by the advent of television. Indeed, even if TV advertising permitted more creative advertising with powerful and dynamic message, its business model was close to traditional advertising channel such as newspaper or radio, selling time slots based on targets defined thanks to demographical criteria. Thanks to digital advertising, a parallel media planning as emerged which integrated, social networking, cloud computing and algorithms (Plummer and al. 2207). Still, the traditional marketing seems to keep focusing on branding and creative contents rather than on data, quantitative models and digital technology (Ha 2008). Stephen J. KIM published an article in the Journal of Advertising research in September 2008 that presents a complete landscape of the advertising in our digital era. According to this paper, besides the implications of advertising professionals in digital medias (mobile, streaming video, gaming, social media, gadgets, etc.) the future of advertising in the digital context is far from clear. Paradoxically, a Microsoft/MTV global study on 14-24 years old individuals demonstrate that if a overwhelming majority has a negative attitude towards advertising (expressing that there is too much advertising in their lives) and rejects the traditional advertising channels by 83%, a majority of the same population welcomes advertising forms that fit theirs needs and their community. As an example of adequate digital

2

advertising, the author highlights the advertising channels used in the PC game Desperate Housewives. In this game, characters interact with branded objects such as CPG beverages or Daimler-Chrysler vehicles. These campaigns offer two positive results: positive qualitative experience for the gamers and a quantitative brand lift for the branded products. According to the author, the success of this type of campaign is based on the added value for the consumer's experience. And, this new success factor leadvertisements to the reconsideration of the evaluation process of media strategies, not only in terms of audience reach and time spent, but by taking into account the consumer's motivation and mindset.

Six characteristics of this digital landscape are highlighted (Kim 2008). First, increasing hardware performance also means that all mobiles devices will become stronger medias for advertising messages to reach targeted audience. Indeed, they will support better graphics, more attractive creative executions, and more complex and engaging applications that will deliver more sophisticated message to consumers.

Second, an always more easy access to the web means that consumers will use this medium more often and more deeply in their everyday life. Therefore, advertisers will enjoy increasing penetration and so increasing opportunities to engage with the consumers

Third, the storage of data on the Internet (through the cloud) and not anymore on individual hard drive will permit unlimited data storage. This aspect will have a huge impact on video-based advertising and on rich creative advertising types. This development will change the consumers' way of consuming information and thus, consuming advertising.

Four, the increased usability of mobile devices thanks to more natural and interactive way of interacting with these device (such as touch screen, voice control…) will create new digital opportunity thanks to the a greater usage of digital devices. This development will slowly open digital advertising to new audiences that were defiant towards digital technologies (i.e. the elderly) or unable to use them properly (i.e. children).

Five, over the past few years, the control of consumers over the content and the displays use (which displays, where and when) has strongly increased. Therefore, mass media are not anymore sufficient in order to reach particular audiences. For digital advertising, the advisers will have to pay great attention to the expectations and the context of a specific digital audience.

Last but not least, digital advertiser should pay attention to the influence of digital communities as the users of social media have evolved from teenagers to white-collars professional.

Marketers have considered for a long time medias as sets of communication channel through which band message were conveyed. In this business model, media institutions appear to be providers of channels to target specific audiences. However, this business model isn't suitable for digital advertising since there are too many communication channels available and a single player cannot planned effectively a media strategy through the communication channels available (Mulhern 2009)

Six principles of digital have been defined (Taylor 2009).

First, as consumers considered their mobile devices as part of their "personal space" and they are very demanding regarding the protection of their privacy (Hart 2008). As a result, the "push" digital advertisements tend to be unsuccessful because they are perceived as an intrusion in the consumer's privacy. Several studies support the idea

that "pull" digital advertisements, when the brands gets a permission before sending any message (Barnes and Scornavacca 2004).

Second, digital advertising acceptance is closely linked to the trust in the advertiser (Barnes & Scornavacca 2004). Moreover, it has also be highlighted that advertisers communicating thanks to digital advertising to consumers that already know them has better results than when communicating to unknown digital audience (Choi 2008)

Third, the digital advertising performances are strongly dependent to the message relevance (Nasco 2008). And, due to the contextualization of every digital advertisement, and because consumers care about their privacy in digital advertising, message relevancy is a key success factor.

Four, as digital advertising offer the possibility to engage for a longer period of time than traditional communication channels (2 to 5 minutes), integrating interactivity in digital campaigns permit to engage deeper with the consumer (McMillan 2003).

Five, in the digital context, entertainment is a major element of digital advertisements. For example, a mini-movie with dramatic elements on an automotive website increased purchase intention as a result of consumers being entertained and staying on the website longer (Raney 2003).

Last but not least, as a major principle, digital advertising needs to take advantage of digital advertising image-building capacity. 'When it comes to building a brand on the internet, never have so many talked so little of what may be the internet's most

stunning capacity – strengthening the brand with customers and prospects.'(Chiagouris and Wansley 2000)

The development of digital advertising has been so strong and fast over the past years consumers have developed a negative attitude towards too intrusive digital advertisements (Truong 2009). The potential long-term of negative attitude towards

intrusive digital advertisements is even considered as equal to potential added value attributed to this new communication channel (Chatterjee, 2008). The instrusive aspect of digital advertising can be stated thanks specific constituents: distracting; disturbing; forced;

interfering; intrusive; and obtrusive (Li, Edwards and Lee 2002). Early studies predicted digital advertising to be less intrusive than television commercials (Rust & Varki, 1996). Indeed, despite potential annoyance produced by internet-based advertisements, they are believed to be more effective in building positive brand evaluation (Sundar & Kim, 2005).

Nevertheless, the perception of digital advertising isn't perceived the same way everywhere (Becerra 2010). The example of the perception of advertising by Hispanic American is a good example to illustrate this reality. Some ethnical specificities in perceiving the advertising were found such as the preference of printed communication channel or the favor of advertisements in Spanish (Chattaraman, Rudd, and Lermon, 2009). Concerning digital advertising, Hispanic Americans would be more sensitive to specific aspects of digital advertisements than the average American population: the language used in the ad , the medium, the perceptions of risk , the reference group influence and the access to the Internet.

The results of the study conducted by Becerra confirm this idea with the following findings: Hispanic Americans have the most positive attitude towards email advertising, followed by banner advertising and then pop-up advertising; pop-up advertising is the least favored type of Web advertising and received the lowest evaluations; attitudes toward pop-up advertising are significantly related to purchases; the influence of subjective norms on online purchase intentions is significant for e-mail advertising only.

Sources

1	Perez, C. 2002. Technological revolutions and financial capital: The dynamics of bubbles and golden ages. London: Edward Elgar Publishing.
2	Mulhern, F. 2009. Integrated marketing communications: From media channels to digital connectivity. Journal of Marketing Communications
3	Plummer, J., S. Rappaport, T. Hall, and R. Barocci. 2007. The online advertising playbook: Proven strategies and tested tactic. New York: The Advertising Research Foundation, Wiley.
4	Ha, L. 2008. Online advertising research in advertising journals. Journal of Current Issues and Research in Advertising 30, no. 1: 31–48.
5	Kim, F. 2008. A Framework for Advertising in the Digital Age. Journal of Advertising Research
6	Taylor, C. 2009. The Six Principles of Digital Advertising. International Journal of advertising 8(3), pp. 411–418
7	Hart, K. (2008) Advertising sent to cellphones opens new front in war on spam. Washington Post, 10 March, p. A1.
8	Barnes, S.J. & Scornavacca, E. (2004) Mobile marketing: the role of permission and acceptance. International Journal of Mobile Communications, 2(2), pp. 128–139.
9	Choi, Y.K., Hwang, J.S. & McMillan, S.J. (2008) Gearing up for mobile advertising: a cross-cultural examination of key factors that drive mobile messages home to consumers. *Psychology & Marketing*, 25(8), pp. 756–768.
10	Nasco, S. & Bruner II, G.C. (2008) Comparing consumer responses to advertising and non-advertising mobile communications. *Psychology & Marketing*, 25(8), pp. 822–838.
11	McMillan, S.J., Hwang, J.-S. & lee, G. (2003) Effects of structural and perceptual factors on attitudes toward the website. *Journal of Advertising Research*, 43(4), pp. 400–409.
12	Raney, A.A., Arpan, l., Pashupati, K. & Brill, D.A. (2003) At the movies, on the web: an investigation of the effects of entertaining and interactive web content on site and brand evaluations. *Journal of Interactive Marketing,* 17(4), pp. 38–53.
13	Chiagouris, l. & Wansley, B. (2000) Branding on the internet. Marketing Management, 9(2),p. 34–38.
14	Truong, Y & Simmons, G. Perceived intrusiveness in digital advertising: strategic marketing implications. Journal of Strategic Marketing. Vol. 18, No. 3, June 2010, 239–256

15	Chatterjee, P. (2008). Are unclicked ads wasted? Enduring effects of banner and pop-up ad exposures on brand memory and attitudes. Journal of Electronic Commerce Research, 9(1), 51–61.
16	Li, H., Edwards, S.M., & Lee, J.-H. (2002). Measuring the intrusiveness of advertisements: Scale development and validation. Journal of Advertising, 31(2), 37–47.
17	Rust, R.T., & Varki, S. (1996). Rising from the ashes of advertising. Journal of Business Research, 37, 173–191.
18	Sundar, S.S., & Kim, J. (2005). Interactivity and persuasion: Influencing attitudes with information and involvement. Journal of Interactive Advertising, 5. Retrieved from http://jiad.org/vol5/No2/sundar/index.htm
19	Becerra, E . 2010. The Influence of Ethnic Identification in digital advertising. Journal of advertising research
20	Chattaraman, V., Rudd, M & Lennon, 2009. "Identity Salience and Shifts in ProductPreferences of Hispanic Consumers: CulturalRelevance of Product Attributes as a Modera- tor."JournalofBusinessResearch